MW01485206

The Crash Signal

The One Signal That Predicts a Stock Market Crash

2nd Edition

By Tim Morris

ISBN: 9781090248213
Published by ZML Corp LLC

Table of Contents

Disclaimer

This book is written for informational, educational, and entertainment purposes only. By purchasing this book, you agree to NOT give any of the strategy presented in this book away in the review section of Amazon. Any reviews with information related to this strategy will be reported to Amazon and deleted.

The creator of this book is not an investment advisory service, a registered investment advisor, or a broker-dealer and does not advise clients on which securities they should buy or sell for themselves. It must be understood that a very high degree of risk is involved in trading stocks. The author and publisher of this book assume no responsibility or liability for trading and investment results.

Investors and traders should always consult with a licensed financial advisor and tax advisor before purchasing any stocks to determine the suitability of an investment. The author receives compensation for the affiliate links used in the book. The Crash Signal is trademarked® and copyrighted © 2021 with all rights reserved. Written by Tim Morris, published by ZML Corp LLC.

About the Author

Hello, my name is Tim Morris. I have been trading and intensively studying the stock market for many years. You could say I'm somewhat obsessed, as I spend most of my free time reading and learning about stocks and economics.

Like most new traders, my initial attempt trading stocks was met with hardship and money lost. I bought all the stupid courses, subscriptions, and books that promised to make me a millionaire overnight. As a shock to many, the courses did not work but instead were filled with hot air and empty promises, the same promises that have littered the internet since the early '90s.

I soon realized get rich quick schemes only benefitted one person, and that would be the person **selling the scheme**. However, knowing the stock market *had* in fact made many people wealthy, I brought it upon myself to learn how so many had used this vehicle of wealth to create income. What I found is there is *no* get rich quick scenario. The stock market can build wealth, but to be an effective trader takes time, and you can't expect instant riches overnight.

I tell you all this to try to give you a little understanding of my material and who I am as a person. I want readers to be able to use the stock market to actually make money, with strategies that actually work. Unlike other authors, I don't sell you pipe dreams. I do my best to give you useful, transparent strategies. Strategies that I use in my own portfolio. Am I the best stock trader in the world? No I'm not. But I've done pretty well, and am confident you can too by using the strategies I present in my books.

To me, it doesn't make much sense to lie to or deceive readers, as that's a pretty poor business model. Sure they may buy one of your books, but *repeat* customers who are happy with your work is the ultimate goal an author can have.

So next time you're surfing the web, and you find someone who tells you they know how to trade like Warren Buffett, turned $1,000 into $1,000,000 in 3 days, or knows how to trade options, stocks, cryptos, forex, futures, and real estate all perfectly and like a pro, be a little skeptical before you decide to give that person your hard earned money.

I enjoy hearing from readers, so if you have any questions while reading this book, feel free to email me at tim@trademorestocks.com. You can also find out more about me, other books I have written, and articles related to stocks on my website TradeMoreStocks.com.

**NOTE: As stated in the disclaimer, please do not place any of this strategy in the review section of Amazon, or your account will be reported to Amazon and your review will be deleted. Thank you.

Introduction

In this introduction, I'd like to go over what is new in the *2nd edition* of this book, as well as what has changed from the *1st edition.*

In the 1st edition I suggested selling all your funds before the market crashed and then buying back in once the market had recovered. As in, I advocated trying to "time" the market using *technical analysis*. Some technical analysis signals have worked okay in the past, but in the most recent crash in 2020 they did not work at all, and you would have lost a lot more money using them versus a simple buy-and-hold strategy.

Selling your entire portfolio while a crash is occurring is *much* easier said than done, especially when you don't have the gift of hindsight to help you. But not only this, by selling all your stocks you run into the issue of paying capital gains taxes, as well as the issue of being wrong and mistiming the crash.

As you may be aware, I am not a big fan of technical analysis, and the more years I spend invested in stocks, the more I realize how big of a sham technical analysis is (as explained in my book *Technical Analysis is Mostly Bullshit*). For this reason, selling your entire portfolio using technical analysis in an effort to "time" the market is not advocated in this book.

No one can time the market perfectly, and anyone who tells you they can is lying; the market is too random. The signal I provide in this book lets you know that a market crash is coming within a specified time period, but it doesn't give you the exact day it will occur. Not only this, no one knows the future and while this signal has predicted crashes for the last 60+ years, it could cease to work one day. For these reasons, I have greatly edited the strategy regarding what to do once The Crash Signal has flashed, what to do when the market is crashing, and how to know when the crash has ended to start investing normally again.

If you happened to read the *1st edition* already, I think you will be very happy with the changes I have made to this book, and will come to find the tools I outline in this *2nd edition* to be a much more effective, easier to follow strategy when an inevitable stock market crash occurs.

Chapter 1
Terminology

Before we get started, there is some terminology we need to go over which will help you understand what is conceptualized in this book. If you're already a pro on stock indexes, ETFs, and moving averages, you can skip this chapter.

S&P 500

The Standard and Poor's 500, commonly abbreviated as the S&P 500, is an index of the 500 largest companies in the US stock market. Because this index is a diverse set of the largest and arguably the best companies in the United States, it is commonly used as a "gauge" of how the whole market is doing. For example, when the S&P 500 is down, many talking heads on TV will say the "market" is down today, and the reverse when the S&P 500 is up.

It's also quite common for stocks which are not in the S&P 500 to correlate with its price movement. As in when the S&P 500 is up, many stocks in the entire stock market are also up on the day. And when the S&P 500 is down, many stocks in the entire stock market are down on the day. It's estimated about 75% of stocks will move the same way as the S&P 500 on any given day, and this correlation tends to increase during corrections and crashes, which is important to recognize for this book.

ETFs

Next we can talk about exchange traded funds, commonly abbreviated as **ETFs**. These are symbols you can buy and sell with your online broker which are actually a number a different stocks "smooshed" together into one symbol. For example, the most common ETF that correlates with the S&P 500 goes by the ticker symbol **SPY**. When you buy SPY, you are essentially buying all the stocks in the S&P 500 at the same time. ETFs originated in the early 1990s and have made a for a very convenient way for the average retail investor to diversify their portfolio.

Most ETFs are "market weighted," in that they allocate more funds towards larger companies in the ETF versus smaller companies. This would be in contrast to "equally weighted" ETFs where all companies, regardless of size, are held at an equal percentage in the fund.

This is all important information to know as the S&P 500 and the ETF **SPY** will be mentioned numerous times throughout this book.

Moving Averages

Moving averages are lagging indicators which show the direction a stock is moving over a specified time interval. They are calculated by taking the closing price of the last "X" number of periods, and then averaging them together to display a line on a chart. This line differs depending on the period and time interval you choose.

For example, say we set up a **50** period moving average on a **daily** chart of SPY. In this case, fifty would the moving average period, and daily, or 1 day, would be considered the time interval. The moving average line would show the closing price of the last 50 days of SPY in the form of a line, continuously updated each day. Had we instead set up this same 50 period moving average on a weekly chart of SPY, it would show the closing price of the last 50 *weeks* in the form of a line. I have an example below of a 50 period simple moving average (SMA) line on a daily chart of SPY.

The two most common types of moving averages are simple and exponential moving averages. Simple moving averages (SMAs) place the same weight on all periods, while exponential moving averages place more weight on more recent stock price movement.

Simple moving averages will be discussed more later in this book.

The 20, 50, and 200 simple moving averages on a *daily* chart are the most common MA lines used by traders.

For those interested, a more detailed explanation of moving averages from Investopedia can be found here: linkpony.com/average.

Chapter 2
Market Crashes

Bad news is an investor's best friend. It lets you buy a slice of America's future at a marked-down price.

- Warren Buffett

You wake up and grab your phone to check the stock market. When you open up your broker, you see the S&P 500 is down 5% on the day. "Oh no" you think to yourself, "is the market crashing?"

This small 5% drop is called a "dip" and tends to occur many times throughout any given year. Dips usually last just a few days and tend to rebound fairly quickly. The next type of drop would be called a "correction," and is defined as a decline of 10% or more from the highs the S&P 500 has made. For example, if SPY closed at $100 today, but in two weeks was priced at $88, the market would be considered to be in "correction territory," as it has dropped over 10% from its highest price point. It typically takes a few weeks to a few months for corrections to fully recover.

And the last type of drop, and the premise of this book, is what is known as a *crash*. This is defined as the S&P 500 dropping 20% or more from its high. Crashes tend to occur rapidly and typically take a few weeks to a few months to initially form, and then can continue trending downward for many months to over a year. Dips and corrections are much more common and *don't usually* turn into a crash.

Unfortunately, without the right insight, market crashes can be devastating to your portfolio. Many traders go through *predictable* market psychology. They see a little 5% drop and don't think too much of it. Then the market is down 10% and they start to get worried. Then the market is down 20%, then 30%, and fear and anger start kicking in. They begin telling themselves, "the market will never recover," "it will keep going down forever," "I don't want to lose any more money," and they end up selling deep into the crash, losing a lot of money in the process. This of course would be the *opposite* of what you want to do, but trading while in a crash versus looking back in hindsight are two very different animals.

On average, a stock market crash occurs every 8 years, however this is just an average. No one knows the exact day a crash will happen, and even the most experienced stock investors and hedge fund managers get caught in crashes. The stock market is one of the best investment vehicles on the planet, but buy and sell at the wrong times, and you can lose a lot more than you make.

For example, had you bought the S&P 500 at the height of the 2000 bull run, you would have lost about 48% of your portfolio in the upcoming crash.

S&P500 – 2000 Stock Market Crash

Then when you finally gained back your money (and sanity) in 2007, you would have had to deal with yet another stock market crash which would have erased over 50% of your portfolio!

S&P500 - 2007 Stock Market Crash

And had you instead invested in the NASDAQ at the height of the dot com bubble in 2000, it would have been even worse! You would have lost over 80% of your money, and it would have taken 17 years *just* to get back to breakeven levels. Talk about a tough time.

NASDAQ- 2000 Stock Market Crash

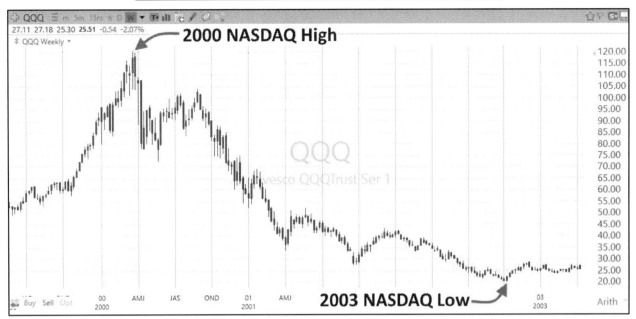

Why does it have to be like this though? Why can't you have your cake and eat it too? What if you could invest in the stock market, reap all the benefits, and know when a crash is coming to prepare and make money from it? I'm here to teach you how to do just that!

As a **token of appreciation** to my readers, I am offering my special report titled *Crush the Market* **absolutely free!** In this report, you will learn 14 incredibly beneficial tips that will help you make money in the stock market. Just type the link below into your browser, put in your email address, and it will immediately be sent to you!

linkpony.com/crush

Chapter 3
The Crash Signal

There is a signal that has preceded every stock market crash since 1956. Within 6 months to 2 years of this signal flashing, a crash has taken place. Before we go over this signal however, we first need to understand the bond market.

Bonds are debt securities issued by a corporation or the government. When an individual buys a bond, they are providing the issuer a specified amount of money in exchange for payment back at a later time *plus interest*. You could classify a bond as a small loan. The bond *yield* is the amount, in a percentage, that you receive in interest on the loan annually. The bond *length* is the amount of time the issuer gets to keep your initial investment.

For example, let's say my company was selling a 3 year bond with a 2% yield. If you gave me $100 today, each year I would provide you 2% in interest (compounded annually), and at the end of the three years you would receive your initial investment back, plus interest, totaling $106.12.

When the government issues bonds, as opposed to a corporation, they are called **treasury bonds**. Different treasury bonds have different lengths of time in which the government gets to keep your original investment. Treasury bond lengths range from 1 month to 30 years. They actually have different names based on the length of time the bond is held, which include treasury **bills** (4 weeks - 1 year), treasury **notes** (2 years - 10 years), and treasury **bonds** (> 10 years). For the sake of simplicity for the rest of this book, I will just be referring to all government issued securities as *treasury bonds*.

Throughout much of history, longer term length treasury bonds have paid more than shorter term length bonds. This only makes sense. If you're letting the government borrow your money for 5 years versus only 1 year, you'd expect a higher rate of return for your money. When the yields of these different length treasury bonds are put onto a chart, they display what is commonly called a "yield curve." Since longer term bonds typically pay more than shorter term bonds, this *yield curve* slowly progresses upward as shown in the graph below.

Normal Yield Curve

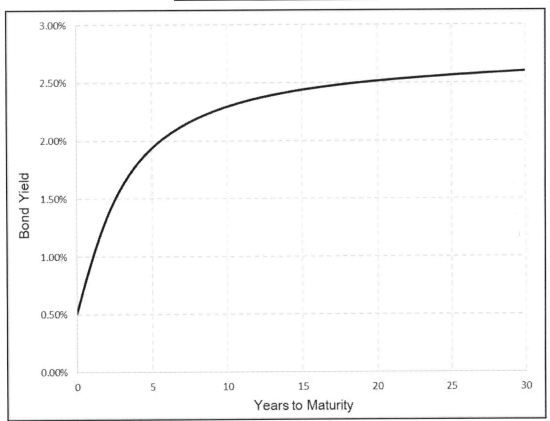

As this graph displays, the greater amount of time the government gets to keep your money, the higher the interest you are paid each year in return. For example, a normal yield curve may show a 1 year treasury bond yielding 2%, while a 5 year treasury bond yields 3%.

However at certain times, bond yields start flattening or inverting. This means the government starts paying you the same amount of interest, or even less interest, for a bond with a longer term time frame, versus a shorter term one. For example, an *inverted* yield curve may show a 1 year treasury bond paying 2.05%, while a 5 year treasury bond pays only 1.95%. Meaning you actually make *more* annually lending your money to the government for just a year, versus had you instead let them hold it for 5 years. The chart below shows an example of what an *inverted* yield curve would look like.

<u>Inverted Yield Curve</u>

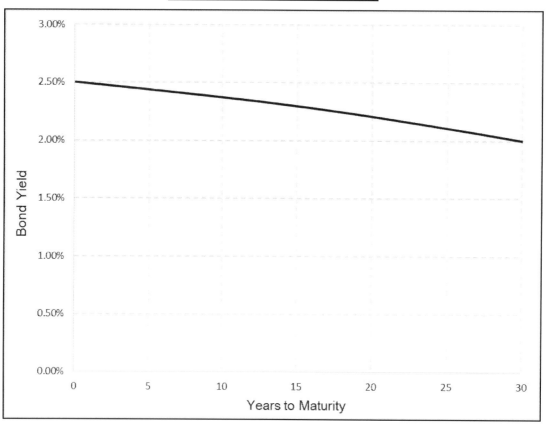

There are many reasons that the yield curve changes which can get complicated. Factors like inflation, Fed rate hikes, supply and demand from investors, and US government fiscal policy all can affect the shape of the yield curve. The key takeaway here though is that the yield curve is a barometer of investors' sentiment towards **the future** of the economy. As such, an inverted yield curve means investors see the future economic outlook as unpredictable, or even poor, compared to the shorter term outlook. For this reason, investors are not willing to lend their money to the US government for an extended period of time, and thus, prices of the shorter term bonds get pushed up higher versus the longer term ones. And it is this *inverted* yield curve that has shown to be an excellent predictor of an economic recession and coming stock market crash for over half a century!

Any time a shorter term bond has a higher yield than a longer term bond, it is a cause for concern. As in, you should start watching the market and monitoring treasury yields more closely. However, there is one inversion metric in particular that is the *real signal* in regards to actually predicting a crash.

Since 1956, every stock market crash has been preceded by an inverted yield curve. From 1956 to 1972, the 1 year treasury bond rising above the 10 year treasury bond had been the relied upon measure to gauge a crash. However, since the 2 year treasury bond was introduced in 1972, the 2yr/10yr yields have become the more favored crossover to watch in regards to predicting a crash.

On the next page is a chart of the 2 year treasury yield plotted against the 10 year treasury yield dating back to June of 1976. The grey vertical shaded areas in the chart indicate when stock market crashes have occurred in the United States. The red circles indicate each time the 2 year treasury yield rose above the 10 year treasury yield.

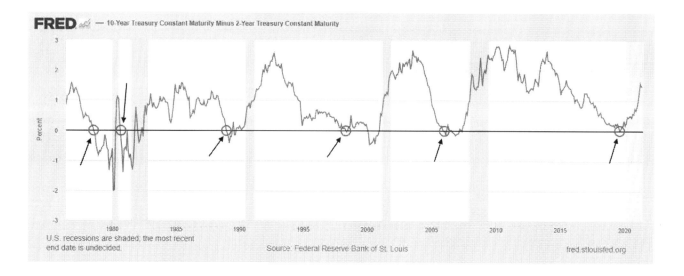

As you can see, shortly after each 2yr/10yr yield inversion (red circles), a stock market crash soon followed. Since 1956, after this signal has flashed, a recession has taken place within 6 months to 2 years, with 20 months being the average.

Let's go over a few specific examples. First, we can look at a chart of the bond yields from 1998, showing the exact day The Crash Signal flashed before the market crash of 2000.

1998 Treasury Bond Yields

Select type of Interest Rate Data
Daily Treasury Yield Curve Rates ⌄ [Go]

Select Time Period
1998 ⌄ [Go]

Date	1 Mo	2 Mo	3 Mo	6 Mo	1 Yr	2 Yr	3 Yr	5 Yr	7 Yr	10 Yr	20 Yr	30 Yr
06/02/98	N/A	N/A	5.08	5.32	5.41	5.53	5.53	5.56	5.62	5.56	5.89	5.80
06/03/98	N/A	N/A	5.13	5.32	5.42	5.55	5.56	5.57	5.63	5.57	5.89	5.80
06/04/98	N/A	N/A	5.12	5.33	5.43	5.58	5.58	5.60	5.65	5.59	5.91	5.82
06/05/98	N/A	N/A	5.12	5.34	5.45	5.58	5.59	5.60	5.63	5.58	5.89	5.79
06/08/98	N/A	N/A	5.16	5.38	5.46	5.58	5.59	5.60	5.63	5.58	5.89	5.79
06/09/98	N/A	N/A	5.17	5.40	5.46	5.60	5.60	5.61	5.64	5.59	5.89	5.79
06/10/98	N/A	N/A	5.14	5.38	5.44	5.55	5.54	5.55	5.58	5.51	5.80	5.70
06/11/98	N/A	N/A	5.11	5.32	5.37	5.45	5.44	5.46	5.49	5.44	5.74	5.65
06/12/98	N/A	N/A	5.13	5.31	5.35	5.43	5.43	5.43	5.48	5.43	5.75	5.66
06/15/98	N/A	N/A	5.16	5.29	5.33	5.43	5.41	5.42	5.45	5.38	5.70	5.61
06/16/98	N/A	N/A	5.20	5.32	5.39	5.50	5.47	5.49	5.52	5.45	5.75	5.65
06/17/98	N/A	N/A	5.23	5.36	5.44	5.55	5.54	5.57	5.61	5.54	5.84	5.74

The chart above is from the government's official website, www.treasury.gov. As you can see, the 2yr/10yr bond yields inverted on June 9th, 1998. This is because the 2 year bond yield (5.60%), moved higher than the 10 year bond yield (5.59%). Let me present to you a chart of the S&P 500, providing a better representation of when the signal flashed versus when the crash actually occurred.

2000 S&P Crash w/ The Crash Signal

As you can see in the chart, 1 year and 9 months after *The Crash Signal* flashed in June 1998, the S&P 500 hit its final high in March of 2000 and the recession started.

Now let me show you a chart of the bond yields from the year 2006, displaying the exact day The Crash Signal flashed before the stock market crash of 2007.

2006 Treasury Bond Yields

Select type of Interest Rate Data
Daily Treasury Yield Curve Rates ⌄ Go

Select Time Period
2006 ⌄ Go

Date	1 Mo	2 Mo	3 Mo	6 Mo	1 Yr	2 Yr	3 Yr	5 Yr	7 Yr	10 Yr	20 Yr	30 Yr
01/19/06	3.98	N/A	4.35	4.47	4.43	4.37	4.32	4.31	4.33	4.38	4.61	N/A
01/20/06	3.95	N/A	4.35	4.48	4.44	4.37	4.32	4.31	4.32	4.37	4.59	N/A
01/23/06	3.98	N/A	4.38	4.50	4.45	4.35	4.31	4.30	4.31	4.36	4.59	N/A
01/24/06	4.24	N/A	4.40	4.51	4.46	4.37	4.33	4.32	4.34	4.40	4.63	N/A
01/25/06	4.22	N/A	4.42	4.54	4.51	4.46	4.41	4.41	4.43	4.49	4.72	N/A
01/26/06	4.17	N/A	4.45	4.54	4.52	4.49	4.45	4.44	4.46	4.53	4.76	N/A
01/27/06	4.19	N/A	4.45	4.55	4.54	4.51	4.46	4.45	4.47	4.52	4.75	N/A
01/30/06	4.18	N/A	4.48	4.62	4.59	4.52	4.47	4.46	4.49	4.54	4.77	N/A
01/31/06	4.37	N/A	4.47	4.59	4.58	4.54	4.49	4.47	4.49	4.53	4.74	N/A
02/01/06	4.33	N/A	4.47	4.60	4.60	4.59	4.54	4.51	4.52	4.57	4.77	N/A
02/02/06	4.32	N/A	4.48	4.62	4.61	4.59	4.54	4.51	4.53	4.57	4.76	N/A
02/03/06	4.31	N/A	4.48	4.63	4.62	4.59	4.54	4.50	4.51	4.54	4.70	N/A

Again, the chart above is from the government's official website, www.treasury.gov. As you can see, the 2yr/10yr bond yields inverted on January 31st, 2006. This is because the 2 year yield (4.54%) moved higher than the 10 year yield (4.53%). Let me again present to you a chart of the S&P 500 which shows when the signal flashed versus when the crash actually occurred.

2007 S&P Crash w/ The Crash Signal

As you can see in the chart, 1 year and 8 months after the *The Crash Signal* flashed in January 2006, the S&P 500 hit its final high in October 2007 and the recession started.

And finally, let's go over the bond yields from the year 2019, which preceded the crash of 2020.

Select type of Interest Rate Data
Daily Treasury Yield Curve Rates ⌄ Go

Select Time Period
2019 ⌄ Go

Date	1 Mo	2 Mo	3 Mo	6 Mo	1 Yr	2 Yr	3 Yr	5 Yr	7 Yr	10 Yr	20 Yr	30 Yr
08/22/19	2.10	2.02	2.00	1.91	1.79	1.61	1.53	1.50	1.56	1.62	1.90	2.11
08/23/19	2.07	2.02	1.97	1.87	1.73	1.51	1.43	1.40	1.46	1.52	1.82	2.02
08/26/19	2.09	2.03	2.01	1.90	1.75	1.54	1.47	1.43	1.49	1.54	1.84	2.04
08/27/19	2.07	2.03	1.98	1.94	1.77	1.53	1.43	1.40	1.44	1.49	1.77	1.97
08/28/19	2.07	2.04	1.99	1.89	1.74	1.50	1.42	1.37	1.42	1.47	1.76	1.94
08/29/19	2.10	2.03	1.99	1.89	1.75	1.53	1.44	1.40	1.46	1.50	1.78	1.97
08/30/19	2.10	2.04	1.99	1.89	1.76	1.50	1.42	1.39	1.45	1.50	1.78	1.96
09/03/19	2.06	2.01	1.98	1.88	1.72	1.47	1.38	1.35	1.42	1.47	1.77	1.95
09/04/19	2.05	2.02	1.97	1.87	1.69	1.43	1.36	1.32	1.40	1.47	1.77	1.97
09/05/19	2.05	2.01	1.97	1.88	1.73	1.55	1.47	1.43	1.51	1.57	1.86	2.06
09/06/19	2.05	2.00	1.96	1.88	1.73	1.53	1.46	1.42	1.50	1.55	1.83	2.02
09/09/19	2.04	1.99	1.96	1.87	1.74	1.58	1.52	1.49	1.57	1.63	1.91	2.11

As you can see, it was in August 2019 that The Crash Signal flashed. And just 6 months later, at the end of February 2020, the stock market crash began, as shown in the image on the following page.

2020 S&P Crash w/ The Crash Signal

For your convenience, I have made a shortened link to the government's official treasury bond page, which is linkpony.com/yield. This page, which is updated daily, displays all bonds with yields from 1 month to 30 years.

I recommend checking this page at least once every couple months to look for The Crash Signal and stay up to date with the yield curve.

Chapter 4
Responding to the Crash

Investors and managers are in a game that is heavily stacked in their favor. Charlie and I believe it's a terrible mistake to try to dance in and out of it based upon the turn of tarot cards, the predictions of "experts," or the ebb and flow of business activity. The risks of being out of the game are huge compared to the risks of being in it.

- Warren Buffett

As mentioned before, any yield curve inversion is significant to note. What this means is if the 1 month yield rises above the 5 year yield, the 3 month yield rises above the 1 year yield, the 1 year yield rises above the 10 year yield, etc. it should worth taking note of. So while the 2yr/10yr yield inversion is the most widely watched by analysts, any treasury bond with a shorter time frame rising above one with a longer time frame should be taken into consideration. So what exactly should you do when you see an inverted yield curve?

When you first see *any* inversion in the yield curve, start monitoring the treasury website more often. You will be keeping a close eye on the 2yr/10yr yields. When the day comes that the 2 year yield rises above the 10 year yield, **The Crash Signal** has officially flashed. Because we don't know *exactly* when the market crash will begin after this signal flashes, it would ***not*** make sense to sell any of your positions at this point. Instead, you now want to start loading up on cash.

Most people invest part of their paycheck each month into their 401K or personal brokerage account. This is of course a great way to build up your portfolio of stocks over time. However, since The Crash Signal has flashed, there will likely be a bear market within 6 months to 2 years, and you want to have money saved to capitalize on the crash. So instead of investing your money into stocks each month as you normally had, you now want to start **saving** the cash you *would have* invested.

While you could place this money under a mattress or into a checking account, a better idea would be to place this cash into your brokerage account to have available when the crash occurs. Many brokers, with Robinhood (*linkpony.com/robinhood*) being one example, pay interest on your unused cash which helps to protect it from the evil enemy known as inflation. Meaning you'll still be making a small return on the unused cash you're not investing.

So again, the plan is to *continue holding* whatever is in your current portfolio, but instead of investing more money into stocks each month as you normally would, you'll now start saving cash.

A crash can take anywhere from 6 months to 2 years to occur once The Crash Signal flashes, with 20 months being the average. In the *1st edition* of this book, I advocated using a technical analysis indicator known as the "death cross" to exit the market in an effort to avoid the crash. This indicator uses a 50/200 simple moving average crossover, and is commonly mentioned by "technicians", talking heads on TV, as well as many authors who write books on the stock market. Let's look at how this indicator worked out for us back in the crash of 2008 with the ticker **SPY**.

Not too shabby huh? The market reached a high of $157 in October 2007, and two months later the death cross got you out of the market at a price of $146. The market reached a low of $67 in March 2009, 15 months after you had exited the market. Here the death cross was quite beneficial and avoided much of the ensuing crash. Now let's again set up this same indicator on SPY, except this time for the 2020 stock crash.

What? That didn't work at all! You would have sold out around $240 in March 2020, exiting with your *entire portfolio* at the very bottom of the crash. As in it was probably the worst thing you could have done. This would have resulted in **a lot** of money lost and **a lot** of taxes paid, effectively negating any money saved during previous crashes.

It's taken me many years to finally realize and admit, but technical analysis is *mostly bullshit*. Trying to sell/buy your entire portfolio in an effort to "time" the market is a loser's strategy that, many times, does not pay off. No one can time the market perfectly, and what ends up usually happening when using technical analysis signals like this is you end up losing a lot more money than you would have made with a simple buy-and-hold strategy. Not only this, let's say you happened to luck out, this signal was somewhat effective like in 2008, and you saved a little bit by implementing it. You now owe Uncle Sam quite a bit of money because of the fact you sold your entire portfolio and have to pay taxes on all the capital gains you incurred.

And, without knowing the future and having a hindsight bias to help you, are you *really* going to sell your entire portfolio in that moment when the market appears to be crashing? It's easy to look at past charts of the market, or for me as an author to tell you about a magical pattern in which you should sell, but try actually being in the crash in real time. Are you going to pull the trigger and actually sell your *entire* portfolio? Much easier said than done. Thankfully, there is a more effective way to take advantage of market crashes which doesn't require so much stress (which I will soon go over).

Along with all the facts I just mentioned, it appears the US Federal Government is responding more quickly to drops in the market, as shown during the 2020 crash. The US government intervening in troubled markets is nothing new, dating back to the Herbert Hoover administration in 1932. But how *fast* they are responding is new. In October of 2008 the Troubled Asset Relief Program (TARP) was passed. This allowed for the US government to directly intervene in the markets by buying shares of stocks of public companies (with taxpayer money I may add). However, this came over a year after the market started crashing. Compare this to 2020 when the Federal Reserve made it known they were printing money and buying bonds in public companies less than *one month* after the crash started. In both these circumstances, soon after the government intervened, the stock market started recovering.

Considering how fast the market rebounded in 2020, and the likelihood the Federal Government will again intervene should a crash occur in the future, technical signals like "the death cross" are unlikely to work like they had in the past. Truly though, no one knows how quickly/slowly future stock markets will crash/rebound, so trying to "time" an exit becomes a loser's game with much more risk than reward, as the Warren Buffett quote at the beginning of this chapter proclaimed.

So instead of trying to time the market in an effort to beat it, a much more effective strategy to employ when a crash occurs is to simply buy the crash on *the way down* with all the cash you have saved.

A bear market is defined as a decline of at least 20% from the market highs. We will be determining when we are in a bear market by looking at the ticker symbol SPY, which is the ETF which correlates with the S&P 500 mentioned in chapter 1.

Taking into account all market crashes since 1956, here are the stats:

Mean	37.00%
Median	35.63%
Avg Length	12 Months
20-29% Crash	4 Times
30-39% Crash	3 Times
40-49% Crash	0 Times
50%+ Crash	3 Times

When we buy into the market during a crash, we want to try to buy-in with the most funds at the most ideal price, while at the same time not missing out on a smaller or larger drop. Without a crystal ball, we of course have no idea where the low of the crash will be. However, based on data from the past, we can formulate a strategy which will provide us a solid return no matter the crash scenario.

This strategy will use a segmented buy-in approach. We will begin to buy-in once SPY has dropped 20% from its highs, and then continue buying in with additional funds at each 5% drop, down to the 50% mark. Here is the outline of this strategy:

Decline	% of Funds Used
20%	25%
25%	20%
30%	20%
35%	15%
40%	10%
45%	5%
50%	5%

As you can see, a larger percentage of funds are allocated at first, with less funds used the greater the market declines. There are three reasons for this:

1. A Deep Crash is Unlikely

Let's say we inverted our allocations, and only 5% of our funds were used when the market declined by 20%, and 25% of our funds were used when the market declined by 50%. This would result in a larger return, but **only if** the market were to decline that low... which it likely ***won't***.

If the market only declined by 20% and then quickly recovered, you basically missed the whole crash, leaving 95% of your allocated funds on the sidelines. Remember, only 3 out of the last 10 crashes dropped below a 39% decline, with a mean and median decline from *all* crashes of around 35%.

So while you *could* obtain a larger return allocating more of your funds to a lower point in the crash, you have no crystal ball to predict the future. And though you will make a little less should there be a large market crash, you won't miss out on a light market crash, which is more likely to occur based on past data.

Not only this, we still have some funds we're allocating towards a deeper market crash. And we actually have more purchasing power the deeper the market crashes, as explained in reason #2.

2. Declines Increase Purchasing Power

The greater the market declines, the greater your purchasing power becomes because of the lowered cost of SPY.

For example, say you have $50,000 in allocated funds and SPY hits a high of $100. You allocate *10%* of your funds for a 20% decline, and *7%* of your funds for a 50% decline.

When SPY drops to $80 (*20% decline*), you're able to buy roughly **62 shares**. However, when SPY drops to $50 (*50% decline*), your 7% allocation allows you to buy **70 shares**.

While not the exact allocations we're using, this example shows that even though we are allocating less of a percentage of our funds to deeper market declines, the *very fact* the market has declined in price increases our purchasing power.

3. You'll Have More Funds With Time

A 40%, or 45%, or 50% decline doesn't happen overnight; it takes time. And a crash isn't happening in a vacuum, as you'll likely still be able to save funds each month as you normally would. Meaning in the many weeks or even months it takes for the market to drop down to deeper levels, you'll have more money saved you can use to add to your allocations. So the 5% allocation you set for a 45% or 50% decline will likely increase in value with the additional cash you are saving while the crash is occurring.

The fund allocations previously listed are of course not an exact science, but instead just based on past data, along with the mean and median of past crashes. Could you tweak these in the heat of the moment during the crash and make more? Possibly... but let's be real... no one knows the future! You're never going to know where the bottom of the crash resides.

Keeping the allocations provided in this book will relay a great return, no matter the crash scenario. Meaning don't get greedy; have a set of rules and stick to the them!

When the market begins declining, start monitoring it more closely. Set an alert with your broker which will go off when the market has declined by 15%. Then, when your alert is triggered, set **all** your limit orders into place at the percentiles mentioned previously, all the way down to the 50% mark. Again, you are not waiting for the market to decline to put in limit orders one-by-one. You are instead setting all your limit orders into place at one time, *before* the market has even dropped to the 20% mark.

Crashes can be stressful and emotional, but having a concrete set of rules in place and setting limit orders beforehand will take out the guesswork and keep you grounded, removing the need to constantly monitor the markets. Let's go over two examples of this strategy in action. The first will be from the crash of 2008.

In this example, The Crash Signal flashed in January 2006, and the market peaked in October 2007. In January 2008, either through our own monitoring or by setting an alert with our broker, we noticed the market dropped 15% from its highs. At this point, we would have put in **all** our in limit orders with the funds we saved since The Crash Signal flashed. In this example, we were able to save $50,000. Here is how our limit orders would have looked:

% Decline	Limit Order	Percent of Funds	Cash Allotted
20%	126.02	25%	$12,500
25%	118.14	20%	$10,000
30%	110.26	20%	$10,000
35%	102.39	15%	$7,500
40%	94.51	10%	$5,000
45%	86.64	5%	$2,500
50%	78.76	5%	$2,500

Let's now look at a chart of SPY showing where our limit orders would have been executed.

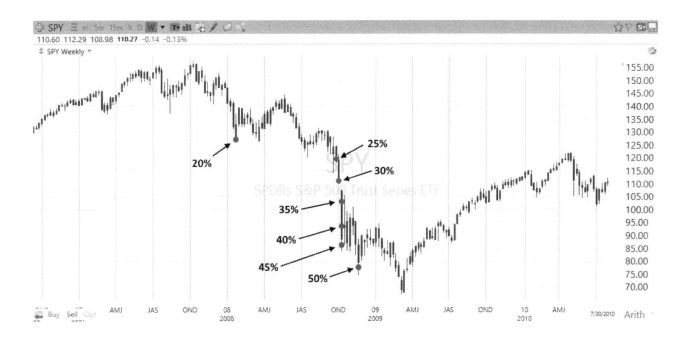

The market peaked in October 2007 at $157.52. Starting in January 2008 and moving to November 2008, all of our limit orders from the table on the previous page would have been executed, all the way down to the 50% mark. The market reached a low of $67.10 in March 2009 before finally reverting higher and recovering. Based on the strategy outlined, our average cost per share would have been $108.39. By the time SPY regained its previous high in March of 2013, we would have realized a 45% profit with 100% of our allocated funds. Let's now go over another example from the crash of 2020.

In this example, The Crash Signal flashed in August 2019, and the market peaked in February 2020. In February 2020, either through our own monitoring or by setting an alert with our broker, we noticed the market dropped 15% from its highs. At this point, we would have put in **all** our limit orders with the funds we saved since The Crash Signal flashed. Again having saved $50,000, here is how our limit orders would have looked:

% Decline	Limit Order	Percent of Funds	Cash Allotted
20%	271.26	25%	$12,500
25%	254.31	20%	$10,000
30%	237.36	20%	$10,000
35%	220.40	15%	$7,500
40%	203.45	10%	$5,000
45%	186.49	5%	$2,500
50%	169.54	5%	$2,500

Let's now look at a chart of SPY from this time period showing where our limit orders would have been executed.

The market peaked in February 2020 at $339.08. Starting in February 2020 and quickly occurring over a period of just one month, four of our limit orders from the table on the previous page would have been executed, down to the 35% mark. The market reached a low of $218.26 in March 2020 before quickly reverting higher and recovering. Based on the strategy outlined, our average cost per share would have been $247.58. By the time SPY regained its previous high in August of 2020, we would have realized a 37% profit (in just 5 months) with 80% of our allocated funds.

Chapter 5
The Market Recovers

Crashes eventually recover, but when they are officially "over" is not a defined science. When a crash is occurring, the market becomes very volatile. One day it may be down 5%, and the next day it moves back up 4%. You may start thinking "oh the market looks good today, let me start buying in again" only for the market to tank again the next day.

While there are no guarantees, there are a few tips to consider to let you know the crash is likely over, and you can start rebuying positions as you normally would.

200 SMA

The first indicator that implies a market crash is likely over is the 200 simple moving average on a daily chart of SPY. Many traders consider a stock to be "bullish" when it's trading above its 200 SMA on a daily chart. This is because a moving average is a lagging indicator, meaning after a crash, SPY would have to be trending upward for a considerable amount of time before it's back above its 200 SMA line.

Rising back above this line implies the market is regaining momentum and recovering, all signs the crash is over. Once SPY has ***closed*** above its 200 SMA line on a *daily* chart for **at least one week**, it becomes a relatively safe time to buy back into the markets. Let's go over an example from the 2020 crash.

As you can see in the chart above, SPY rose above its 200 SMA in May 2020, and while a little volatile, the market did eventually recover, making this a safe place to have gotten back into the market.

This 200 SMA strategy has worked during all crashes since *The Crash Signal* started

(1956), except for the dot com crash of 2000. While the market was going through the dot com crash, it rose above its 200 SMA line in 2002 for about 2 weeks, before proceeding to fall another 30%. Besides this one occurrence though, this strategy has worked very well.

Golden Cross

An even safer strategy to consider which *has* worked after every market crash since 1956 is known as the *golden cross*. This is where the 50 SMA line on a daily chart of SPY crosses *above* the 200 SMA line. This is another lagging indicator, but lags even further behind SPY itself moving above its own 200 SMA. And while there is less reward, as you're waiting a longer amount of time for the market to recover, there is also less risk, considering this strategy has yet to fail after a crash. The picture below shows where the golden cross has occurred following all three crashes since 2000.

Government Policies

And finally, watching for government policies which will benefit the markets can also help you determine when a bottom will occur. There tends to be three major categories government policies fall into.

Fed Funds Rate

The "Fed Funds Rate" has a large impact on the yield curve, the stock market, and the economy as a whole. This is the interest rate the Federal Reserve sets, which coincides with the far left side of the yield curve. When the Fed lowers this rate, money becomes "easier" to borrow as mortgages, consumer loans, and credit from banks comes with a *lower* interest rate. Economic theory states this will encourage consumer spending, which in turn will help the economy recover. For this reason, the traders tend to like when the Fed lowers rates, as it's generally bullish for the stock market.

In 2001, when the market started crashing, the Federal Reserve began slashing the Fed Funds Rate in an effort to prop up the stock market. From 6% in the year 2000, they slashed it down to 1% by 2003, at which point the market finally recovered and began rising.

After the dot com crash, the Fed Funds Rate was slowly increased over the coming years, rising back to 5.25% by 2007. However in 2008, when the financial crisis occurred, the Fed again cut rates, slashing them all the way down to 0% in 2009.

It took many years, but the Fed slowly raised the Fed Funds Rate up to around 2.50% by 2019. However in 2020, when the market started crashing, the Fed immediately cut the Fed Funds Rate back down to 0% in an effort to help the economy.

In all these circumstances, the Federal Reserve slashing interest rates was part of the catalyst which ending up stimulating the economy and helping the market recover. And while it's not an immediate fix, it is one metric to watch during crashes to indicate that a recovery is on the horizon.

Congressional Bills

At the end of 2008, the federal government signed into law a bill called TARP which allowed for the US government (with tax payer dollars) to buy mortgage backed securities, as well as shares of many different companies in the stock market. Many of the companies that were helped (with tax payer dollars), were the same companies that actually *caused* the financial crisis (but I digress). Five months after this bill was signed into law, the market found a bottom and recovered.

In March of 2020, Congress signed into law a bill known as the CARES Act. This $2.2 trillion dollar bill sent direct payments to citizens of the United States, allowed small businesses to receive forgivable loans, and even allocated $500 billion dollars to give to large corporations.

Just the news of this bill getting passed caused a rebound in the market, which ended up finding a bottom a week *before* the bill was signed into law.

Federal Reserve Intervention

The Federal Reserve is another branch of the government which tends to try and improve the economy during recessions. Besides the Fed Funds Rate, there are other tactics they employ which can spur a recovery in the market. During the dot com crash

(2000-2003), the Fed responded by lowering interest rates as well as providing more liquidity to banks.

In November 2008, during the financial crisis, the Federal Reserve announced they would expand their balance sheet to help the market. This strategy by the Fed has come to be known as "quantitative easing," which is where the Fed prints money out of thin air to inject into the markets. They ended up spending $800 billion dollars buying corporate debt, making emergency loans, and purchasing mortgage backed securities. And do note, this was a *separate* $800 billion dollars than the TARP bill signed by Congress.

In March 2020, during the corona crash, similar policies were employed by the Federal Reserve, except this time they *directly* intervened in the markets by also buying corporate bonds. Instead of just $800 billion however, this time they raised their balance sheet by $3 trillion dollars.

All these examples show that soon after the US government starts signing bills or the Federal Reserve turns on their money printer, the market soon recovers. And it appears they are now responding much quicker than they did in the past, with 2020 being a good example, as both Congress and the Federal Reserve responded in less than a month's timeframe to the ensuing crash.

And to be clear, I am not advocating for the US government or the Federal Reserve to spend taxpayer money frivolously, or print money from thin air while our country is already trillions of dollars in debt. What I am saying though is these policies do appear to work, as injecting money into the market ultimately raises stock prices and decreases the rate of a downtrending market. Meaning government intervention is something to look for during a crash, as history has shown markets tend to recover soon after the government begins intervening.

Chapter 6
Additional Considerations

So far, we've just been buying SPY when the market has crashed. This of course may not be how everyone wants to partake in crashes, as you may have a particular stock you think will have a higher return on investment. In this case, I would still use SPY as your guide of *when* to buy in, as opposed to watching the chart of the particular stock you want to purchase. As in, when SPY moves down 20%, 25%, etc., at those points you would want to purchase your intended stock.

The reason for this is some stocks, especially those most affected by the cause of the crash, end up declining at a greater rate. For example during the dot com bubble in the 2000s, tech stocks had the biggest declines. During the financial crisis in 2008, bank stocks took a huge fall. And during the coronavirus crash of 2020, travel stocks were the hardest hit. However, no matter the scenario, the general market is going to be the driving force for when *everything* moves back up. And because of this, you can likely get the stock you want at a better price using SPY as your guide. Let me go over an example to better explain this point.

Say you thought Delta Airlines (DAL) was oversold during the 2020 crash and you wanted to buy into it. You of course *could* have bought Delta with the outline presented before, as in at a 20% drop, 25% drop, etc. However, as stated in the previous paragraph, travel stocks were the hardest hit, meaning they were declining at a greater rate than the general market. Let me show you in a side-by-side chart.

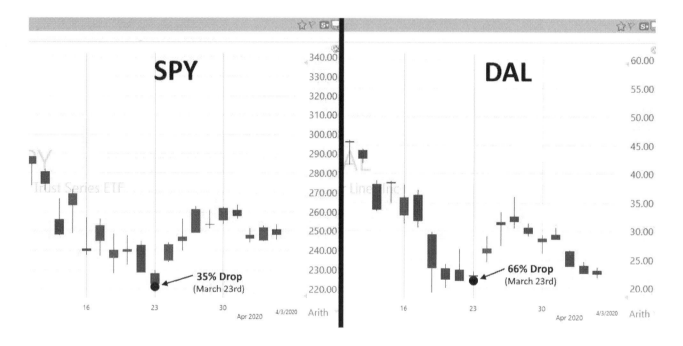

Here you'll see on March 23rd, SPY was down to $219, a decline of 35% from its highs. On this same day Delta was down to $21, a decline of **66%** from its highs. This was actually the bottom of the crash, and the S&P 500 soon moved higher, taking Delta and the rest of the market with it. Using SPY as your guide, you would have been able to buy into Delta at much better price points, including near its absolute bottom.

So should you choose to trade other stocks during a crash, use SPY as your guide of when to buy-in, which will likely allow you to get into these stocks at a better price.

Shorting

Shorting the market may seem like a good idea during crashes, as you can make money as the market is declining. The issue is you can't time the market. One day the market could be declining, and the next day the government enacts a policy that causes the market to skyrocket. No one knows when the final bottom will occur, so I would say if you do decide to short stocks during a market crash, use a *very small* amount of money. And don't get greedy! If you make some money, close your positions and be happy with your profits.

Leveraged ETFs

Similar to shorting, leveraged ETFs are rather risky to buy, and this is especially true during crashes. For those unfamiliar, leveraged ETFs are symbols which move up or down at a *multiple* of non-leveraged ETFs. For example, UPRO is a 3x leveraged version of SPY. So when SPY moves up 1%, UPRO moves up 3%. This of course implies the reverse is also true, meaning you can lose 3x your money.

Again, you don't know where the bottom of the market will be, and should the crash go on for a while after you buy into a leveraged ETF, you would end up losing a lot of money.

Another issue with leveraged ETFs is something known as contango. It's basically where the leveraged ETF loses value just from price fluctuations in the underlying stocks it's attached to.

And lastly, leveraged ETFs can simply disappear in value overnight, especially during periods of extreme volatility (*e.g.* crashes), like in the case of SVXY back in 2018.

For all these reasons, my suggestion would be similar to shorting, in that if you decide to buy a leveraged ETF during a crash, use a very small amount of money and don't get greedy.

Chapter 7
Review of Strategy

Now that you know exactly what The Crash Signal is and the steps to take when a crash occurs, let's go over a summary of this strategy that you can reference in the future.

1. Monitor Treasury Yields

At least once every couple months, use this shortened link which will take you right to the US Treasury's website (*linkpony.com/yield*). Here, you will be looking at the yields of all the shorter term treasury bonds, to check if any have risen above a *longer* term bond. If one has, check back to this website more often and start more closely monitoring the 2yr yield versus the 10yr yield.

2. The Crash Signal Has Flashed

Once the 2yr treasury yield has risen above the 10yr treasury yield, The Crash Signal has flashed. You will now start saving the cash you *would have* invested each month. Put this saved cash into a brokerage or savings account (preferably one that pays interest).

3. Monitor the Market

Typically it takes anywhere from 6 months to 2 years once The Crash Signal has flashed for a market crash to occur. Start monitoring the market more closely, as you're watching for SPY to fall at least 15% from its high. Some stock brokers or charting software, with TC2000 being an example, allow you to set alerts in your account to let you know when a ticker symbol has fallen a specified amount. You would want to set an alert at a 15% drop from the high of SPY to let you know the market is nearing bear market territory.

4. Start Buying

Once the market has fallen at least 15% from its highs, you will now set **all** your limit orders into place. You of course can buy whichever stocks you want, but a safe strategy would be to just buy SPY. The limit order allocations are outlined in the table below.

20% Decline - 25% of Funds
25% Decline - 20% of Funds
30% Decline - 20% of Funds
35% Decline - 15% of Funds
40% Decline - 10% of Funds
45% Decline - 5% of Funds
50% Decline - 5% of Funds

5. The Crash is Over

While a crash is occurring, the government will likely start enacting policies in an effort to "help" the economy. You're looking for the Federal Reserve to lower interest rates, and/or market intervention from Congress and the Federal Reserve. This should start to set in motion a recovery. Then you will wait until either SPY has closed above its 200 SMA line on a daily chart for *at least* one week, or until the golden cross appears. These two indicators let you know that the crash has likely ended, and you can start investing into the markets as you normally would. The golden cross has less reward, but is also less risky versus the 200 SMA.

6. Sell for a Profit

The best time to sell SPY, or another stock you bought during the crash, is when it reaches its previous high. This takes out the guesswork and gives you a nice easy target you can stick to.

Once the golden cross has occurred on a daily chart of SPY, set a limit order at SPY's previous high to sell your entire position. Now you no longer have to watch the market and your limit order will execute automatically for you once SPY reaches its previous high.

But of course, if you want SPY or another stock you purchased during the crash to be in your long-term portfolio, you will instead just hold indefinitely.

If you are enjoying this book, could you please leave a review on Amazon? It would be greatly appreciated and allow me to come out with more informative books in the future. A shortened link to the review page is below:

linkpony.com/crash

Final Thoughts

You make most of your money in a bear market, you just don't realize it at the time.

- Shelby Cullom Davis

When the market is going through a crash, it can be a very scary time. You start thinking about all the worst case scenarios in regards to the economy, how long the crash will last, how low the market will go, etc. Try to calm down your emotions by taking a look at the history of the United States stock market and recognize that markets recover! It may take some time, but the market **will** recover and it **will** regain its highs. The stock market is a *long-term* investment with great outcomes for those who actually hold long-term.

And now, by using the strategy outlined in this book, you have a plan to take advantage of the crash. And having a solid plan, one which you can stick to, will allow you to avoid making the mistakes so many other traders tend to make during crashes, as well as make a considerable profit from it.

I hope you enjoyed this book and were able to gain some useful knowledge. If you have any questions, feel free to e-mail me at tim@trademorestocks.com. To learn more about me, as well as more valuable information about the stock market, check out my website at TradeMoreStocks.com.

If you enjoyed this book, you may also like:

How to Beat the Market

A Simple Long-Term Investment Strategy that Beats the S&P 500

Shortened Link to Book:

linkpony.com/beat

Learn how to beat the S&P 500 by an average of **3.12%** per year! These returns are achieved *without* leverage, options, or excess risk... just pure, regular old stocks. Not only this, you *don't* even have to pick the stocks… all that is taken care of for you! All you have to do is rebalance your portfolio once a year... that's it. This is truly the **best** long-term stock strategy I have ever discovered (which is why I use it in my own portfolio). Find out more at the link above **right now!**

Technical Analysis is Mostly Bullshit

Why Flipping a Coin Is a Better Strategy than Using Technical Analysis in the Financial, Stock, and Forex Markets

Shortened Link to Book:

linkpony.com/ta

Give me 5 minutes of your time, and I'll show you how looking at lines on a chart will make a millionaire... *sound familiar*? In *Technical Analysis is Mostly Bullshit*, Tim first goes over the theory, and then shows you why technical analysis is as fictional as Santa Claus or the Tooth Fairy in the financial markets. When you're done reading this book, you'll realize why technical analysis is simply astrology for men in their 30's. Find out more **now** at the link above!

The 20% Solution

A Long Term Investment Strategy that Averages 20.13% Per Year

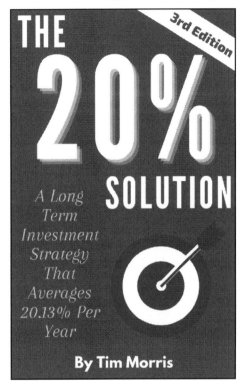

Shortened Link to Book:

linkpony.com/20

You read that right, **20.13% per year!** This strategy, which I have coined *The 20% Solution*, requires just 4 trades a year. And of those 4 trades, very little is destined to capital gains tax. This book includes 30 years of history of this strategy in action, with charts and figures. Go to the link above to find out more

Manufactured by Amazon.ca
Bolton, ON

25372351R00039